Science to the Rescue

Dry in the Desert

Can science save your life?

Gerry Bailey

Crabtree Publishing Company
www.crabtreebooks.com

Crabtree Publishing Company
www.crabtreebooks.com
1-800-387-7650

PMB 59051, 350 Fifth Ave.
59th Floor,
New York, NY 10118

616 Welland Ave.
St. Catharines, ON
L2M 5V6

Published by Crabtree Publishing in 2014

Author: Gerry Bailey
Illustrator: Leighton Noyes
Editor: Shirley Duke
Proofreader: Kathy Middleton
Production coordinator and
   Prepress technician: Tammy McGarr
Print coordinator: Margaret Amy Salter

Copyright © 2013
BrambleKids Ltd.

Photographs:
All images are Shutterstock.com unless otherwise stated.
Cover - Zelijko Radojko; nutsiam; anson;
prochasson frederic; Rafal Cichawa Pg 1 - Zelijko Rado-
jko Pg 2/3 - Zelijko Radojko
Pg 6/7 -Anton Balazh; Joingate
Pg 9 - Michael Freeman/Corbis Pg 11 –
(t)Images of Africa Photobank / Alamy (m) National
Geographic Image Collection / Alamy (b)LOOK Die
Bildagentur der Fotografen GmbH / Alamy Pg 12 -
Loskutnikov Pg 13 - funkyfrogstock Pg 14 - James Michael
Dorsey Pg 15 – (t) Dr Ajak Kumar Sing (b) Seleznev
Oleg Pg 16/17 - Sergei25 Pg 17 – (l)Cat Downie (r)James
Michael Dorsey (b)Kavram Pg 18 - Patrick Poendl Pg 19 -
vvroe Pg 20/21 - Rafal Cichawa
Pg 21 – (l) Rob Roeck (r) Rosa Frei(b)anson
Pg 22/23 - Victor Paul Borg / Alamy
Pg 23 - Photononstop / Superstock
Pg 24/25 - Kubais Pg 25 – (t)Rafal Cichawa
(b)Jaap Berk The Netherlands
Pg 26/27 - Ergeny Murtola
Pg 26 – (t) Clara(b)CharmeleonsEye
Pg 28/29 - Sunsinger Pg 28 – (t)James Michael Dorsey (b)
James Michael Dorsey
Pg 30/31 - Zelijko Radojko
Pg 30 – (t) Prochasson fredric(b)Sunsinger
Pg 32 – (t)apdesign (b)nutsiam
Camel Frieze - Sergej Rozvodovski

Printed in Canada/032014/BF20140212

Library and Archives Canada Cataloguing in Publication

Bailey, Gerry, author
       Dry in the desert / Gerry Bailey.

(Science to the rescue)
Includes index.
Issued in print and electronic formats.
ISBN 978-0-7787-0429-4 (bound).--ISBN 978-0-7787-0435-5 (pbk.).--
ISBN 978-1-4271-7541-0 (html).--ISBN 978-1-4271-7547-2 (pdf)

       1. Deserts--Juvenile literature. I. Title.

GB611.B35 2014   j551.41'5   C2014-900922-4
                                           C2014-900923-2

Library of Congress Cataloging-in-Publication Data

CIP available at Library of Congress

Contents

Joe's story

Hi, it's Joe here.
I've got an exciting story to tell.
It's about an adventure I had
in the **desert**.

I got lost in a **sandstorm**. While I
looked for shelter, the swirling
sand covered my jeep, and I couldn't
find it under the huge **dunes**.

The desert is a sea of sand out
there and it's hot. Very hot!
I managed to survive though,
with the help of the science I
know and my **Tuareg** friends.

So grab a cool drink, settle down
and I'll get started.

My story is set in a hot desert. A desert is a huge stretch of rock and sand that often looks like an empty wasteland. Only a few kinds of plants and animals can survive there.

There are deserts in many places of the world, but I was in one particular desert— the Sahara. I was hunting for something special—a lost city!

What is a desert?

A desert is an area on Earth's surface that receives less than one inch (2.5 cm) of rain each year. The ground is dry, and the few plants that grow are able to store the water they need.

How hot is it?

Temperatures are measured using a thermometer placed in the shade and out of the wind. The hottest reading ever recorded on Earth was 136°F (57.8°C) in 1922 in northern Libya. BUT the ground surface can get much hotter than the air. A NASA satellite recorded a surface temperature of over 150°F (70°C) in the desert in Iran.

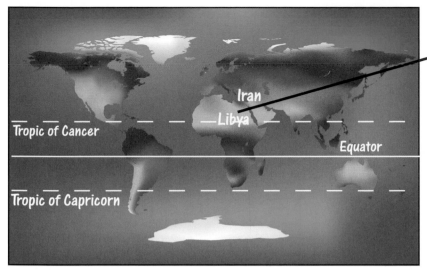

The Sahara is one of the largest deserts on Earth. It stretches across the northern part of Africa.

The equator is the name given to an imaginary line that runs around the middle of the planet. Many hot deserts are located along the Tropic of Cancer and the Tropic of Capricorn. These two imaginary lines circle the globe above and below the equator. They mark the boundaries of an area known as the tropics—the warmest part of the planet.

In the Sahara, the average rainfall is less than two inches (five cm) a year, and in some areas there is no rainfall at all for years at a time.

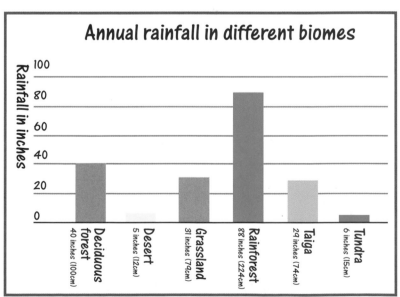

Annual rainfall in different biomes

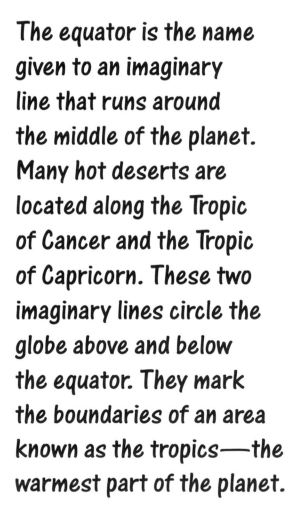

All was going well until the sandstorm hit. It blew up suddenly, and I had to stop because my jeep had no roof or windows. I climbed out to see if I could find shelter ahead. By the time I turned back, the jeep was gone—buried under the sand! I had no idea where it was.

Dusty winds

Strong winds often blow over desert areas. Not only do they produce sand dunes, but they can lift sand into the atmosphere creating dangerous sandstorms. They block out the sun and bury roads and oases.

Harmattan—In the Sahara, the harmattan is a very hot wind that blows clouds of red dust.

Khamsin—The khamsin is a hot, dry wind that blows across the Sahara to Egypt. It lasts about fifty days in the spring. A cold, dusty one sometimes blows in winter.

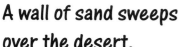
A wall of sand sweeps over the desert.

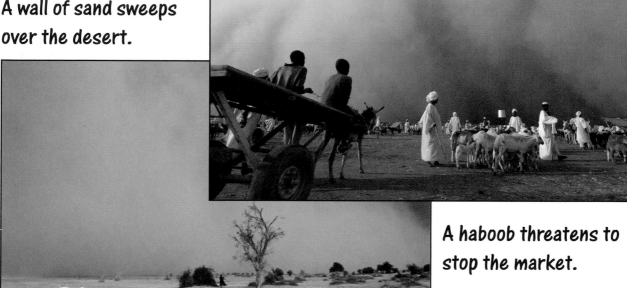

A haboob threatens to stop the market.

Sirocco—The sirocco is a hot wind that carries dust, grit, and sand across the Mediterranean Sea to Italy, Greece, and Turkey. It can pick up enough dust and sand to produce sandstorms.

Haboob—The haboob is a strong wind that causes sandstorms in the southern areas of the Sahara. It is usually followed by thunderstorms and even small tornadoes. A haboob usually lasts for around three hours and can carry large quantities of sand that move in a dense wall. The wall of sand can reach up to 3,200 feet (1,000 m) in height.

The storm passed, but I no longer knew where I was. The desert track had vanished, along with the jeep.

Which of the piles of sand covered it? This one? That one?

I climbed the highest mound of sand, hoping I would find a clue. These dunes, as they are called, are constantly blown along. They form curved shapes and ridges, and even stars, across the land.

But amazingly, it wasn't all sand. I could see water. A great stretch of it glimmering in the distance.

What is a dune?

In sandy deserts the wind piles the sand into high ridges called dunes. The dunes form different shapes and have different names.

Barchan dunes can move quickly, up to 328 feet (100 m) a year.

Barchans are the most common dunes. This dune is even found on Mars. They have a crescent shape with horns pointing in the direction of the wind. They are created by winds that blow in one direction.

The long lines of linear dunes can be spotted from space.

Linear dunes are much longer than they are wide. They form ridges that run parallel to the wind and each other. Linear dunes can be 525 feet (160 m) long.

China has star dunes that are 1,640 feet (500 m) tall.

Star dunes look like huge starfish in the desert. They have ridges, or arms of sand, that spread out from a central mound. They are created by winds that blow from different directions.

I wanted to believe it! I was really thirsty, and there, right before my eyes, I could see a large lake.

But I'm a scientist, and I knew this was just a **mirage**—a trick of the light.

Mirages

A mirage is caused by the bending of light by air as it travels. Light travels in a straight line, but it travels faster through warm air close to the ground than it does through cooler air above.

As light passes from warm to cooler air, it bends. You are tricked into thinking your eyes are seeing something straight ahead. However, the bent light reaches your eyes from a different place than where it began. It can make a far object look like it's in a different place than it really is, or reflect blue sky onto the desert making it look like there is a lake.

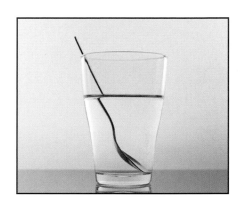

Light moves at different speeds through different materials. It moves more slowly through water and glass than it does through air. When light slows down or speeds up, it bends in a new direction. This bending, called refraction, makes the spoon look divided.

sunlight

reflected sunlight

cool air

refracted sunlight

hot air

false image

13

It was time to get some rest. The sun sets quickly in the desert. The air cools off quickly, too. There is little moisture in the atmosphere to block sunlight during the day. The lack of moisture allows the heat to escape rapidly at night.

I quickly put up my tent and settled in for the night.

Portable homes

Homes that are carried from place to place need to be portable. Moveable homes have different shapes and use different structures. Tensile structures are formed by stretching a cover over posts stuck into the ground.

Awassi sheep once roamed the Syrian desert. Farmers raise them for meat, milk, and wool.

Tents like this one are used by the Bedouin and Tuareg peoples of the Sahara. They are erected like this.

Modern nomads

Today, the lifestyle of the Bedouin is changing. Trucks are taking the place of camels as the main method of transportation. Some camps have refrigerators and television sets powered by portable generators. Coffee is brewed for guests on gas stoves rather than the traditional hearth, the place for gathering around the fire. Canvas tents are almost as common as goat-hair homes.

Bedouin homes have not changed for about 4,000 years. Short wooden posts are sunk into the sand to support a framework of tightly stretched goat-hair ropes. A loosely woven goat-hair fabric is stretched over the ropes to act as the walls and roof.

I was kept awake by the sound of little feet scurrying around the tent. Many desert animals are nocturnal— they're active at night when it's cool.

So I became nocturnal, too. I set off in the moonlight to follow their trails. Maybe, I thought, they'll lead me to water.

What animals live there?

Very few mammals live in the desert, since most cannot store water and survive the heat. Small animals use camouflage to hide among the rocks and sand.

An addax

The body of the Fennec fox has features that help it keep cool in the desert. Extra-large ears allow it to release heat from its body rapidly. Its pale coat reflects the hot sunlight. It has special kidneys that help reduce the loss of water from its body.

The main Sahara camel is the one-humped dromedary. Camels store fat in their humps, which their bodies break down into nutrition and water when they must go without food for a long time. They also have special kidneys that help them go without water for long periods of time.

The addax is an antelope that has flat feet, which help it walk across the sand. The animal's large size makes it slow-moving, so it is easy prey for poachers. There are very few left in the wild today, and they are in danger of becoming extinct.

The region's mountains are the natural habitat of the ibex. The ibex is a tough goat that is able to survive on scarce plant life.

And they did! After a while I spotted the tops of palm trees and knew I had reached an **oasis**. And I was positive the water would be fresh and cool.

My water bottle was empty, and I was thirsty.

I drank and drank. Then I filled my water bottle.

What is an oasis?

An oasis is a spring where water from an **aquifer**, or an underground supply of water, comes to the surface. The spring provides fresh water for plants and animals. People and animals in the Sahara depend on the oases and remember their locations.

Trade caravans need to travel from oasis to oasis to restock supplies.

Deep wells are dug to reach the water trapped in the aquifer.

Aquifers

Aquifers occur where water is trapped in a layer of permeable rock, sand, or gravel. Permeable means the rock has spaces where water can seep in. When every space in an aquifer is filled with water, it is called a saturated aquifer. The highest level of the saturated area is known as the water table. The water table will rise or fall depending on rainfall.

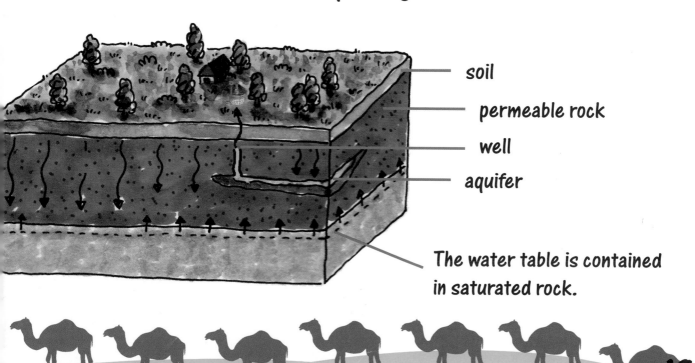

soil

permeable rock

well

aquifer

The water table is contained in saturated rock.

If the oasis had been dry, there were plenty of plants around it. Most desert plants store water in their roots and stems. When things get really hot, they can use this supply. And I could have done the same thing!

Much refreshed, I satisfied myself with a large handful of dates that hung from a nearby palm. They were good!

Plants of the deserts

The North American brittlebush plant grows tiny hairs on its leaves. These hairs protect the plant from heat and cold, acting like a kind of blanket. They also help trap moisture.

The date palm has been a source of food for thousands of years. The date is the fruit of the palm and provides energy. It's easy to store and carry on long journeys in the desert.

Cactus spines are the leaves of this plant. Spines lose less water during the hot day than flat leaves.

I rested in the shade and must have dozed off. When I opened my eyes, I thought I was dreaming.

I could see a wall in the distance. Could it be true? Yes! I had come across the ancient settlement I was looking for. This region had once been rich farmland and not desert. Before me was the ruins of one of the many cities that thrived here long ago.

22

Garama

About 3,000 years ago, a great civilization flourished in the Sahara. It was the Garamantes civilization, and it lasted many hundreds of years.

This region had once been fertile, but as the desert started to spread across the land, the Garamantes people knew they had to find more water to survive. These remarkable people invented a network of tunnels called **foggaras** to reach the underground aquifers and get water for drinking and irrigation.

Water allowed them to grow crops such as grapes and wheat. Their population grew and cities sprang up. However, after removing nearly 36 million gallons (136 million liters) over 600 years, the water began to run out. Today only ruins of this great civilization survive.

Foggara ditches still bring water to the desert.

The ruins of the capital city, Garama, lie in present-day Libya.

Expanding deserts

Desertification describes how deserts spread, taking over more fertile land. This is happening in parts of the Sahara where there have been longer dry spells over the past few decades. The result is that crops don't grow and food and water become scarce.

Scientists believe that the main reasons for expanding deserts are animal grazing and clearing the land for logging. Both activities pull up plant roots, which causes soil erosion. Oil and other mining in the desert pollutes water and kills plants. Once damaged, the dusty soil can take centuries to recover.

In many parts of the world, water must be carried to homes the hard way!

24

A modern foggara

In Libya, a great pipeline known as the Great Man-Made River (GMR) is being laid across the desert. It is the world's largest irrigation system.

A total of 1,800 miles (2,820 km) of pipeline and aqueducts bring water from freshwater aquifers deep below the Sahara. The water is drawn from more than 1,300 wells, most over 1,640 feet (500 m) deep. It supplies water to cities throughout Libya.

Moved by the wind, the sand slowly invades fertile land and plants quickly die.

Each day the GMR supplies millions of gallons (liters).

Although I now had water and dates, I really needed to find my jeep and restock my supplies. Luckily, help was at hand!

Tents are easily set up and taken down when people move.

I heard the loud honk of a camel and was surprised to see that a group of Tuareg traders had arrived at the oasis. They greeted me and offered me tea and fruit.

They told me stories of Garama and how it had once been a great city. Then I told them all about the sandstorm and my lost jeep.

The tribespeople of the Sahara enjoy hosting gatherings.

26

Who lives in the desert?

There are two main tribes in the Sahara. The Bedouin are Arabs who came into the area from the Middle East. They speak Arabic. The Tuareg are **Berber** people from the coastal Mediterranean regions of northern Africa. The Tuareg language is one of the Berber languages.

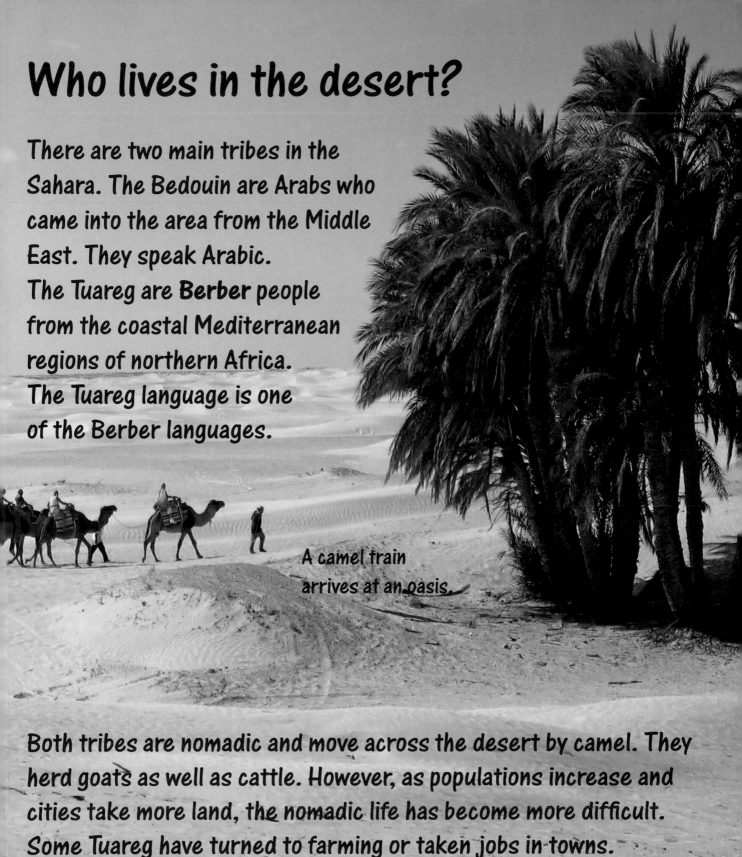

A camel train arrives at an oasis.

Both tribes are nomadic and move across the desert by camel. They herd goats as well as cattle. However, as populations increase and cities take more land, the nomadic life has become more difficult. Some Tuareg have turned to farming or taken jobs in towns.

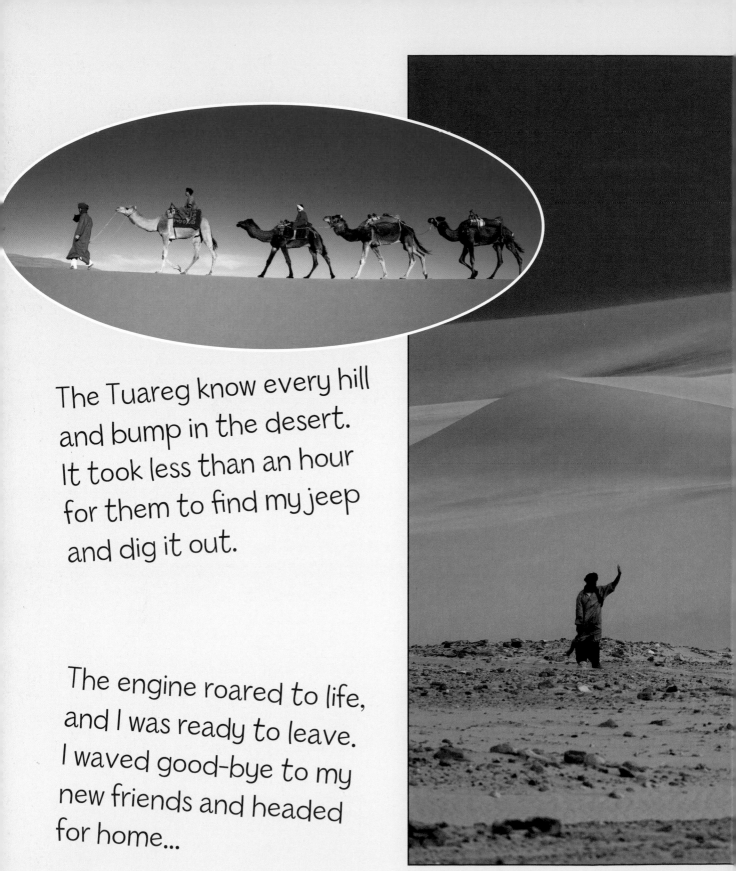

The Tuareg know every hill and bump in the desert. It took less than an hour for them to find my jeep and dig it out.

The engine roared to life, and I was ready to leave. I waved good-bye to my new friends and headed for home...

Glossary

aquifer
Formed when water is trapped under the ground in a layer of porous, or permeable, rock, sand, or gravel

barchans
Crescent-shaped sand dunes

Bedouin
An Arab people who came originally from the Middle East. Traditionally, the Bedouin are nomads, moving their herds from place to place in search of food. Today they are more settled traders.

Berber
A people that originated in the coastal region of North Africa. They are also traditional nomads.

desert
Any area on Earth that gets less than one inch (2.5 cm) of rain a year

desertification
The process by which desert areas of the world expand

dunes
Moving mounds of sand blown by the wind into different shapes. The most frequent shapes are barchan, linear, and star-shaped.

foggaras
Networks of tunnels built to reach underground aquifers to provide water

haboob
A strong, southern Sahara wind that is often followed by thunderstorms or tornadoes

mirage
An optical illusion that occurs when light, moving through warm air near the ground, bends. It makes objects appear to be in a different place than where they actually are.

oasis
A spring where water from underground seeps to the surface. The water allows plants to grow.

sandstorm
A storm that occurs when winds blow sand and dust into the atmosphere

Tuareg
A Bedouin people known by their indigo-blue turbans and face covering.

Learn More...

Books:

Desert Survival Guide
by Ruth Owen.
Crabtree Publishing Company, 2010.

Camels
by Melissa Gish.
Creative Paperbacks, 2013.

Bedouin: Nomads of the Desert
by Alan Keohane.
Kyle Cathie, 2008.

Websites:

Learn desert survival skills:
http://www.desertusa.com/desert- activity/desert-survival-skills.html

Find out interesting facts about different deserts around the world:
http://www.factmonster.com/ipka/A0778851.html

Learn about the way of life of the Bedouin people:
http://www.dakhlabedouins.com/by_bedouin_life.html

Index